Great Napkin Folds

Great Napkin Folds

Gay Merrill Gross

CRESCENT BOOKS
NEW YORK ● AVENEL, NEW JERSEY

A FRIEDMAN GROUP BOOK

This 1994 edition published by Crescent Books, distributed by Outlet Book Company, Inc., a Random House Company,
40 Engelhard Avenue, Avenel, New Jersey 07001.

Random House
New York ● Toronto ● London ● Sydney ● Auckland

ISBN 0-517-10303-6

SIMPLY SENSATIONAL:
GREAT NAPKIN FOLDS
was prepared and produced by
Michael Friedman Publishing Group, Inc.
15 West 26th Street
New York, New York 10010

Editor: Elizabeth Viscott Sullivan
Designer: Stephanie Bart-Horvath
Art Director: Jeff Batzli
Illustrator: Steven Arcella
Photography Editor: Christopher C. Bain

Color separations by Rainbow Graphic Arts Co., Ltd.
Printed and bound in China by Leefung-Asco Printers Ltd.

9 8 7 6 5 4 3 2

In memory of my father,
an artist, storyteller, and craftsman

Acknowledgments

I would like to thank the many wonderful members of The Friends of The Origami Center of America. In particular, I thank my dear friend, the late Lillian Oppenheimer, for broadening my knowledge in the folding arts. I would also like to express my appreciation to the creative staff at the Michael Friedman Publishing Group: Elizabeth Sullivan, editor; Jeff Batzli, art director; Steven Arcella, illustrator; and Stephanie Bart-Horvath, book designer.

To the best of my knowledge, all designs used in this book are traditional, unless credited.

Contents

© Michael Grand

$\mathcal{A}$ beautifully set table immediately establishes a mood and sends a welcoming message to your guests. Whether you are setting the table for a casual get-together or an elegant dinner party, napkin folding is a fun and creative way of dressing up a table.

Folding napkins into decorative shapes is surprisingly simple. If you can fold a shirt, tie a bow, and pleat a paper fan, you already have all the necessary skills.

The history of napkin folding can be traced back at least as far as the sixteenth century, when elaborately folded cloth creations adorned the banquet tables of Renaissance Italy. Although drawings of these intricate cloth representations of animals, birds, and full-rigged ships have been recorded, the folding patterns are not known. In the mid-nineteenth century, books on household management gave instructions for several decoratively folded napkin designs. These folds were far less complicated than the highly complex pleated creations of earlier years, as they employed clever folding techniques to create appealing table ornaments with a minimum of effort. Many of these patterns, such as the Water Lily (see page 54), have become classics.

Great Napkin Folds contains classic napkin folds as well as newer designs. Just choose a fold that coordinates with your table setting and is appropriate for the occasion. For success with folded napkins, here are some pointers to keep in mind:

- The napkin designs in this book are arranged in order of difficulty. If you are new to napkin folding, try the folds near the beginning of the book first. For a quick glance at all of the designs, check the picture index at the back of the book.

- Before trying the designs, study the "Symbols Used in This Book" and "Basic Folds" sections on pages 11 and 14. If an instruction is not clear to you, look ahead to the next drawing, as it will show you the result you are trying to achieve.

- When purchasing new cloth or paper napkins, buy square ones. Most napkin designs require perfectly square napkins.

- Choose a design that is suitable for the type of napkin you are using. A standing or intricately folded design works best from a linen, cotton, or cotton-blend napkin. If your napkins are limp, they may also require a little starching. An all-polyester napkin does not take a crease well, so any folds you make will not hold in place. For this type of material, use a design that is held together with a napkin ring or glass; any spreading effect may actually be beneficial for such a design.

- You can create interesting effects by using different-colored napkins that are folded together as one.

- Look for unusual accessories to coordinate with your folded designs: real and artificial flowers and interesting napkin rings, such as colorful ribbons, braided cord, tassels, or costume jewelry.

- Napkin folding will be more fun and relaxing if you don't leave it to the last minute. Napkins for a party can be folded hours or even a day ahead of time.

- You need not reserve napkin folding for formal affairs or company. Make everyday meals a little more special with the added touch of a pretty napkin fold. This will also give you good practice for company.
- Create your own variations on the designs in this book. Experiment with a napkin by rolling, pleating, or draping it into interesting forms. If you like the design you have created, keep a sample folded from a paper napkin so you can recreate the design at another time.

Whether you want to create a conversation-starter or to add a nice finishing touch, napkin folding is an inexpensive and enjoyable way to create a memorable table setting.

Symbols Used in This Book

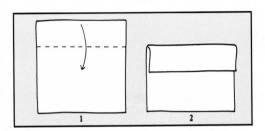

A line of dashes means to fold forward or toward you.

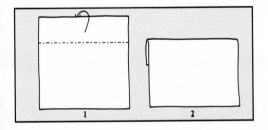

A line of alternating dashes and dots means to fold backward or away from you.

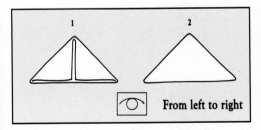

From left to right

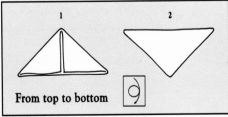

From top to bottom

A looped arrow means to turn the napkin over in the direction of the arrow.

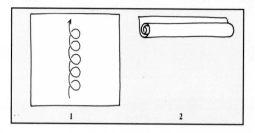

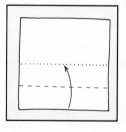

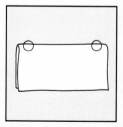

An arrow with multiple loops means to roll the napkin in the direction of the arrow.

A dotted line indicates a hidden or imaginary line that is used as a reference mark.

A circle indicates a place where you should grasp the napkin.

13

Basic Folds

Each napkin design will begin with either a completely open napkin or one of these basic folds:

BOOK FOLD (In Half)

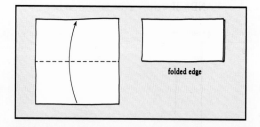

folded edge

1. Begin with an open napkin. Bring the bottom edge up to meet the top edge, folding the napkin in half.

2. Position the folded edge of the napkin as directed in the instructions.

LETTER FOLD (In Thirds)

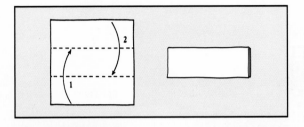

1. Begin with an open napkin. Fold the napkin in thirds, as if folding a letter.

2. Completed Letter Fold.

HANDKERCHIEF FOLD (In Quarters)

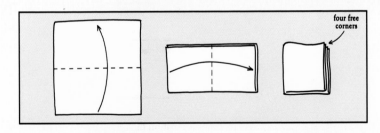

1. Begin with an open napkin. Fold the napkin in half.

2. Fold in half again.

3. Completed Handkerchief Fold.

Napkin Designs

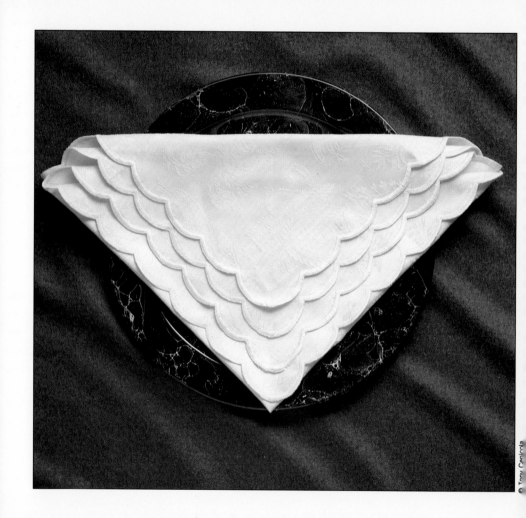

Lovely Layers

Use a napkin that looks good on both sides for this pretty design.

Begin with a square napkin folded into quarters, like a handkerchief.

1. With the four free corners at the top, lift the first top corner and fold it down to the bottom corner.

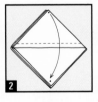

3. Individually fold down the third and fourth top corners in a similar manner to create four distinct layers that are evenly spaced apart.

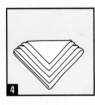

2. Lift the second top corner and fold it down to lie slightly above the previous corner.

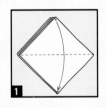

4. Completed Lovely Layers. Place it on the table as is or add a few folds to create a variation such as the Seashell design on page 20.

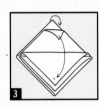

Seashell

This decorative design will look nice on your table any time of the year!

Begin with a napkin folded into Lovely Layers (page 18).

1. Turn the napkin over from left to right.

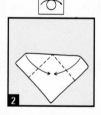

2. Place a finger at the center of the top edge. Fold the top right and left corners down so that they meet in the middle and a point is formed at the top.

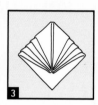

3. Place the Seashell on a plate. The layers on each side can be fluffed up slightly.

21

© Tony Cenicola

Ribboned Roll

Elegance and simplicity characterize this easy-to-do fold. Its likeness to a diploma makes it particularly suited for a graduation party.

Begin with a napkin folded in half, like a book.

1. Fold the top corners down to form a point at the top.

3. Tie a ribbon around the roll or insert the roll through a napkin ring.

2. Roll the bottom edge upward to the top point.

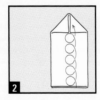

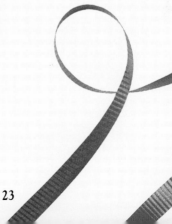

24

Lover's Knot

This design is inspired by the secret love letters of years past. The letter was tied into a knot, to be opened and read by the loved one alone.

Begin with an open cloth napkin.

1. Fold the top corner down to the bottom corner.

2. Beginning at the bottom corners, roll the napkin up from bottom to top.

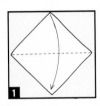

3. Loosely tie the roll into a knot.

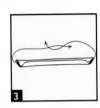

4. Completed Lover's Knot.

Ruffles

The soft folds of this pleated design create a lovely ruffled look to dress up your table.

Begin with an open napkin.

1. Beginning at the bottom edge, accordion-pleat the napkin up to the top edge.

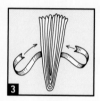

3. Slip the folded end of the napkin through a ring or tie a ribbon around the middle of the pleats.

2. Place the right and left ends of the napkin together, folding the pile of pleats in half.

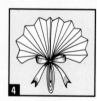

4. Fan out the pleats for your completed Ruffles.

27

Silverware Holder

The Silverware Holder offers a sleek package to contain each guest's eating utensils. It provides an interesting touch for a sit-down meal and a convenient package for the buffet table. Use a napkin that looks good on both sides.

Begin with a napkin folded in half, like a book. The folded edge is at the bottom.

1. There are two layers at the top edge of your napkin. Loosely roll the front layer down to the middle of the rectangle.

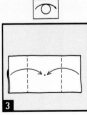

2. Flatten the roll into a wide band running across the middle of the napkin. Holding the band in place, turn the napkin over to the back side.

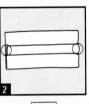

3. Fold the side edges inward to meet at the middle.

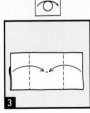

4. Fold the napkin in half as shown.

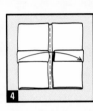

5. Put the silverware into the outside pocket.

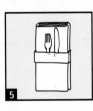

29

30

This simple design will create a dramatic effect with minimal effort.

Begin with a napkin folded into quarters, like a handkerchief.

1. Place the four free corners at the top. Fold the bottom corner up approximately one-third of the way between the bottom and top corners.

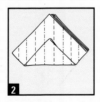

2. Starting at one side corner, accordion-pleat the napkin to the opposite side corner.

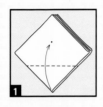

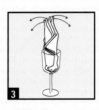

3. Insert the bottom of the napkin into a drinking glass. Separate the four layers at the top of the napkin.

4. Gently shape the petals of your finished flower.

Pointed Pocket

This fold features a deep pocket that can hold silverware, chopsticks, breadsticks, or a flower. Use a napkin that looks good on both sides.

Begin with a square napkin folded into quarters, like a handkerchief.

1. Place the four free corners at the top. Lift the first top corner and fold it down to lie slightly above the bottom corner.

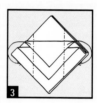

3. Fold the side corners behind to overlap on the back of the napkin.

2. Fold the second top corner down to lie slightly above the corner of the first layer folded down.

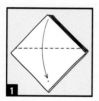

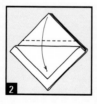

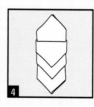

4. Completed Pointed Pocket.

This versatile fold features a slit that can be purely decorative or put to good use. Slide a name card into the opening or insert a dinner roll to keep it warm.

Begin with an open square napkin. The side that you want to show should be face down.

1. Fold the four corners inward to meet at the center. Adjust the folds so that all the newly formed corners are sharp.

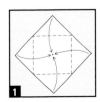

3. Fold the napkin in half from right to left.

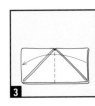

2. Gently lift the center of the left and right side edges and fold the napkin backward, in half.

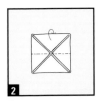

4. Completed Split Square.

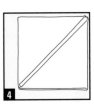

Tri-Fold

This handsome fold will lend a distinctive look to your table setting.

Begin with a napkin folded into thirds, like a letter.

1. Fold in the right and left sides to form a border approximately 2 inches (5cm) wide on each side.

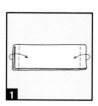

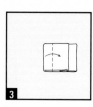

3. Fold the left side toward the right so that each of the folded edges on the right are the same distance apart.

2. Fold the left side toward the right, so that it overlaps the open edges of the right border.

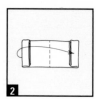

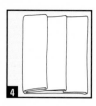

4. The completed Tri-Fold can be placed in a horizontal or vertical position.

37

Butterfly

(Design by the author)

The Butterfly works best when made from a cloth napkin.

Begin with a napkin folded in half, like a book. The folded edge is at the top.

1. Fold the top corners down to meet at the middle of the bottom edge.

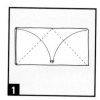

2. Fold the slanted sides inward to meet at the center.

3. Fold the top point backward to meet the two points already at the bottom.

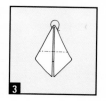

4. Push the right and left sides backward until they meet.

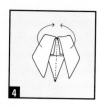

5. Bring the right and left bottom points up as far as they will go.

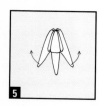

6. Fold the bottom point under the rest of the napkin. Softly shape the completed Butterfly.

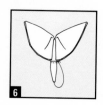

39

Candy Cane

Vary the colors of this simple-to-make design to match the holiday or occasion. You will need two paper or cloth napkins in contrasting colors.

Begin with both napkins fully open.

1. Place one napkin over the other, leaving a V-shaped border, approximately 1 inch (2.5cm) wide, at the bottom.

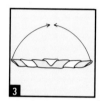

3. Bring the right and left ends of the roll together, loosely folding the roll in half.

2. Starting at the bottom corner, roll both napkins together toward the top corner.

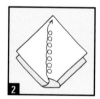

4. The finished Candy Cane can be inserted into a glass or draped across a plate.

41

Standing Fan

Fine restaurants and cruise ships often adorn their tables with this beautiful design.

Begin with a napkin folded in half, like a book.

1. Beginning at the bottom edge, accordion-pleat the napkin two-thirds of the way toward the top edge.

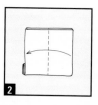

2. The pleats you just made should be behind the bottom edge. Fold the napkin in half from right to left; the pleats should now be on the outside.

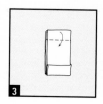

3. Fold the top edge of the napkin down to form a narrow hem.

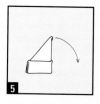

4. Fold the left side of the napkin down diagonally and tuck it behind the pleats. (If this edge does not fit neatly behind the pleats, go back to step 3 and adjust the size of the hem you made.)

5. Stand the napkin on its right edge.

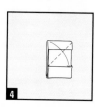

6. Release the pleats to form the completed Standing Fan.

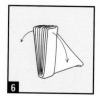

43

Tuxedo Fold

This elegant design suggests the tucks and folded layers of a formal cummerbund. Use a napkin that looks good on both sides.

Begin with a napkin folded into quarters, like a handkerchief.

1. Place the four free corners at the top right. Lift the corner of the first layer and loosely roll it diagonally down as far as it will comfortably go (just past midway). Flatten the roll into a narrow band.

2. Lift up the second free corner and fold it backward on a line slightly above the first band. Adjust this fold to create a second band, equal in width and parallel to the first.

3. Repeat step 2 with the third layer, creating a third band equal in width to the first two.

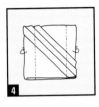

4. Fold the right and left sides to the back.

5. Completed Tuxedo Fold. The pockets behind each band can be used to hold silverware, a flower, or a name card.

VARIATION: After step 3, position the napkin as shown and fold the side corners to the back.

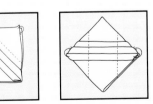

Triangle Blocks

Triangle Blocks are compact packages that are easy to handle. If you fold several in a variety of colors, they look attractive in a stack, or can be laid out in a tiled or layered pattern.

Begin with an open napkin. The side that you want to show should be face down.

1. Fold the top and bottom edges inward to meet at the center.

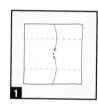

4. Fold the slanted edge created in step 3 down so that it lies directly over the long bottom edge.

2. Bring the top edge down to the bottom edge, folding the napkin in half.

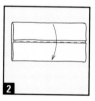

5. You have created an equilateral triangle at the left side of your napkin. Fold the left edge up to lie directly over the long top edge.

3. Imagine an invisible line at the horizontal center of the napkin. Fold the bottom left corner up to this line, forming a sharp angle at the top left corner.

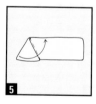

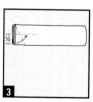

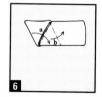

6. Continue in this manner, adding layers to your equilateral triangle two more times.

7. (a) Fold down a small triangle at the top right corner. (b) Tuck the bottom right corner into the pocket formed by the layers of the large triangle.

8. Completed Triangle Block.

48

Triangle Blocks (p. 46)

© Tony Cenicola

Pretty Points (p. 50)

49

Show off a decorative napkin with the Pretty Points design.

Begin with a square folded into quarters, like a handkerchief.

1. Position the napkin so that the single folded edge is at the right and the four free corners are at the bottom left. As you lift up corner A, hold the lower three in place. Take corner A to the far right to form a large triangle as shown in the next drawing.

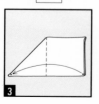

2. Carefully turn the napkin over from left to right.

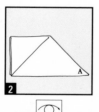

3. Place a finger at the left corner of the top edge. Lift the first corner at the bottom right and gently pull it to the far left, forming a triangular shape.

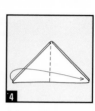

4. Fold the napkin in half from left to right.

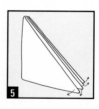

5. Slightly spread the layers apart to show off each individual point.

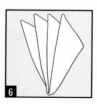

6. The completed Pretty Points can be placed on the table with the points up, down, or to the side.

The soft wavy frills make this a delicate and graceful design. Use a napkin that looks good on both sides.

Begin with a napkin folded into quarters, like a handkerchief.

1. With the four free corners at the top, lift the first top corner and fold it down to the bottom corner.

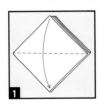

2. Lift the same layer you just folded down and accordion-pleat it four times to appear as in the next drawing. Adjust the pleats so that they are even.

3. Hold the pleats in place with one hand or place a drinking glass over them. Lift the next layer at the top of the napkin and pleat it four times to mirror the pleats created in step 2.

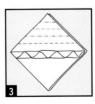

4. Holding all of the pleats in place, carefully fold the right half of the napkin back behind the left half.

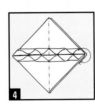

5. Rotate the completed Fancy Frills to the position shown in the photograph.

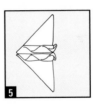

52

Fancy Frills (p. 51)

© Tony Cenicola

© Michael Grand

Water Lily (p. 54)

The layers of petals and lovely flower shape have made the Water Lily
a traditional favorite.

*Begin with an open square napkin. The side that you want to show should
be face down.*

1. Fold the four corners inward to meet at the center.

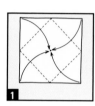

2. Fold the four new outside corners inward to meet at the center.

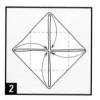

3. Again, fold the four new outside corners inward to meet at the center.

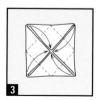

4. Holding the four flaps securely in place, carefully turn the napkin over.

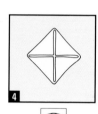

5. Fold the four corners inward to meet at the center.

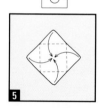

6. Hold the center points tightly in place for steps 6 through 10. Starting at one outside corner, slip your free hand underneath the napkin and pull out one of the loose corners from the underside.

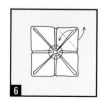

7. Gently tug this corner upward until it softly wraps around the other point like a high-backed collar.

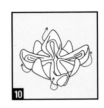

10. Reach under each petal from the first layer to find another loose point. Carefully pull each one out and gently tug it upward to give the flower a cup shape.

8. Repeat steps 6 and 7 on the remaining corners of the napkin. Remember to hold the center points firmly in place.

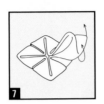

11. Completed Water Lily. As well as being a beautiful decorative fold, its cuplike shape can be used as a container.

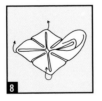

9. Slip your free hand under the napkin and find a loose point that lies between two petals. Pull the point out and gently tug it upward. Repeat three more times.

VARIATION: If you are using a small paper napkin, omit steps 3 and 10. Your Water Lily will have eight petals instead of twelve.

Cracker Holder

This very clever design turns a cloth napkin into a useful container for crackers, wrapped candy, sugar packets, or other table fare.

Begin with a large cloth napkin folded into thirds, like a letter.

1. Turn the napkin over.

4. Reach under the flap you just folded over and unfold the flap you folded over in step 2.

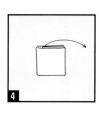

2. Fold the right side edge to the center. (This is a temporary fold that serves as a guide for the next step. It is unfolded in step 4.)

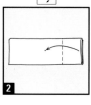

5. Lift the top folded edge of the flap and fold it down one-third of the way. As you do this, the top left corner will squash down and form a small triangle (see drawing 6).

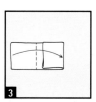

3. Fold the left edge over to the far right edge.

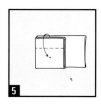

6. Repeat step 5 at the bottom of the flap.

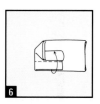

7. You now have a narrow flap extending from two small triangles. At the base of the triangles, fold the flap over to the left.

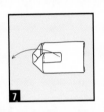

8. Fold the right edge of the napkin over to the left edge of the narrow flap.

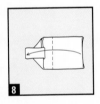

9. Repeat steps 5 through 7 on the right side.

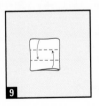

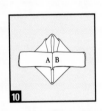

10. Grasp edges A and B and turn the napkin inside out. The flaps that are now extending out to the sides will fall inside and line a rectangular-shaped basket.

11. Completed Cracker Holder. Shape the basket by pressing your fingers into the bottom corners and straightening the sides and lining.

Cracker Holder (p. 56)

Rose (p. 60)

Rose

(Collected by Stephen Weiss)

Turn a plain paper napkin into this pretty flower. Use the Rose as a table decoration or favor.

Begin with an open paper napkin. If the napkin is three-ply, separate the layers and fold a Rose from each.

1. At the left edge, fold over a hem approximately 2½ inches (6cm) wide.

4. Bring the top edge down and up again, winding the hem end around four fingers.

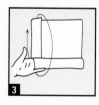

2. Curl up the bottom edge of the napkin and wrap the hem edge once around the index finger of your left hand. Hold it in place with your middle finger.

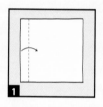

5. If the hem end is not yet completely wound around the four fingers of your left hand, continue winding it loosely until the napkin is completely rolled up.

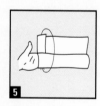

3. Grasp the left side of the top edge of the napkin and bring it down and up, winding the hem end around three fingers.

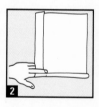

6. With your right hand, tightly pinch the napkin at the tips of your left fingers. Holding the pinch firmly, remove your left hand.

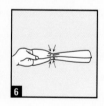

7. With both hands, continue to pinch the napkin at the base of the flower; then begin twisting a stem under the flower by tightly pinching the napkin and twisting your hands in opposite directions. (The secret to a successful stem is to pinch and twist as tightly as you can, without tearing the napkin.)

8. Continue twisting the stem until you are one-third of the way down the length of the stem. Then find the loose outside corner at the bottom of the stem end. Gently pull this corner and lift it up until the tip of the corner reaches the flower. This will form the leaf of the Rose.

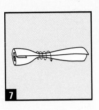

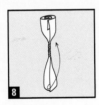

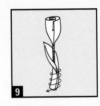

9. Tightly pinch the base of the leaf and continue twisting until you reach the bottom of the stem.

10. Completed Rose.

62

This fold is based on a traditional Japanese origami design. It is sure to delight and impress your guests.

Begin with a napkin folded in half, like a book.

1. Fold the top edge backward to form a narrow hem approximately 1 inch (2.5cm) wide.

4. Fold the top edge backward. It should lie approximately in line with the bottom of the triangle.

2. Fold the right and left top corners down to meet at the middle, forming a triangle.

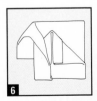

5. There are two folded edges at the top of the left side. Separate these edges and fold the front layer over to almost the center of the napkin.

3. While holding the top triangle in place, fold the bottom edge behind and above the triangle, making a crease slightly below the bottom of the triangle.

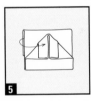

6. At the top of the separated layers is a loosely formed, irregular triangle. Flatten this triangle to appear as shown in drawing 7.

7. Repeat steps 5 and 6 on the right side.

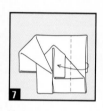

8. Fold the top edge and part of the irregular triangles backward so that the fold you create is directly behind points A and B.

9. Lift up the right and left sides of the center collar and tuck the nearby edges of the Kimono under them.

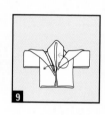

10. Completed Kimono.

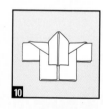

64

Sachet

The intricacy of this design will intrigue and impress your guests. Choose a napkin that looks good on both sides.

Begin with an open napkin.

1. Fold the napkin in thirds, as shown, so the open edge is on top.

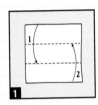

2. Take the first layer of the top edge and fold it down twice to form a narrow band across the center of the napkin.

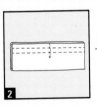

3. Holding the napkin at each side to keep the band in place, carefully turn the napkin over.

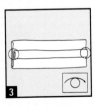

4. Fold the right and left sides inward (approximately one-sixth of the way).

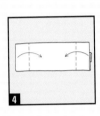

5. Fold in each side to meet at the center.

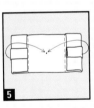

6. Fold the right side of the napkin backward so that it lies under the left side.

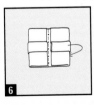

7. Place a finger from each hand behind the first layer of the top edge. Pull one finger down to form a small diamond shape with a slit down its center. Flatten this shape evenly and tuck the bottom point under the band. Repeat at the bottom of the napkin.

8. Completed Sachet.

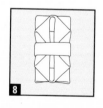

67

Picture Index

Butterfly • 38

Candy Cane • 40

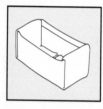

Cracker Holder • 56

Fancy Frills • 51

Kimono • 62

Lovely Layers • 18

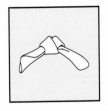

Lover's Knot • 24

Petals • 30

Pointed Pocket • 32

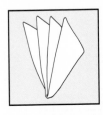

Pretty Points • 50

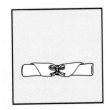

Ribboned Roll • 22

Rose • 60

Ruffles • 26

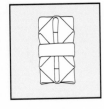

Sachet • 65

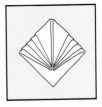

Seashell • 20

Silverware Holder • 28

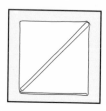

Split Square • 34

Standing Fan • 42

Triangle Blocks • 46

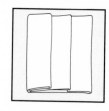

Tri-Fold • 36

Tuxedo Fold • 44

Water Lily • 54

Index